One is tempted to splash about in an Andrew Neil Blewitt waterfall of wit, whimsy and wordplay and then exclaim "More foibles than Aesop!".

But that would merely underline the futility of trying to keep up with a bountiful bard in full flight.

This sophisticated successor to *A Millipede with Gout* confirms instant impressions of a master at ease with the most unlikely of material and always ready to give the familiar a fresh coat of appealing paint.

Limericks, nursery rhymes, Bible stories, favourite poems, famous people, annoying habits, endearing traits, Test Match Special, The Farmer's Boy... they all get the Blewitt blessing along with a key revelation that laughter is a great wrinkler. Just put a trunk call through to any elephant with a sense of humour.

Then, as he glides effortlessly from playful to pensive, Andrew turns on the power and poignancy in a series of moving poems. Such contrast adds extra value to a volume of vibrancy and rich imagination.

One is tempted to suggest that if Dragonflies Have a Problem, perhaps it's because they spend too long on the wing and so feel like committing insecticide. Then again, it can be wise to resist temptation.

Keith Skipper MBE, DL, Norfolk writer, broadcaster and entertainer.

Andrew Neil Blewitt's comic verse is a delight, frequently laugh-out-loud funny. And yet as this collection makes clear, he can move 'from playful to pensive' in a way that is reminiscent of Longfellow and Kipling. *Dragonflies Have a Problem* is by turns hilarious and poignant.

Professor Andrew Cowan, Director of Creative Writing
School of Literature, Drama and Creative Writing,
University of East Anglia

www.andrew-cowan.com

ANDREW NEIL BLEWITT

1930–2009

With his ready wit and puckish delight in human foibles, Neil enjoyed turning his thoughts into humorous verse. Early retirement gave him the chance to indulge in his long-held wish to write. He constantly honed his skills and polished words and nuances. He once said, "A poem is never finished; it is always a matter of negotiation."

He read widely and with great enjoyment. He admired the verbal dexterity of Nash and Gilbert and the punning of Hood. He felt in tune with the humanity of Cowper and Hood, while his battered copy of Longfellow's works was a constant companion.

Dragonflies Have a Problem

Also by Andrew Neil Blewitt

A Millipede with Gout

ANDREW NEIL BLEWITT

Dragonflies Have a Problem

Vanguard Press

VANGUARD PAPERBACK

© Copyright 2015

Andrew Neil Blewitt

The right of Andrew Neil Blewitt to be identified as author of
this work has been asserted by him in accordance with the
Copyright, Designs and Patents Act 1988.

A CIP catalogue record for this title is
available from the British Library.

ISBN: 978-184386-965-8

Cover illustration by Ed Norden

*Vanguard Press is an imprint of
Pegasus Elliot Mackenzie Publishers Ltd.*

www.pegasuspublishers.com

First Published in 2015

**Vanguard Press
Sheraton House Castle Park
Cambridge England**

Printed & Bound in Great Britain

Acknowledgements

With thanks to all those people who, albeit unwittingly, provided inspiration and to John Robinson for help with computer work.

ONE CHEER FOR THE LOSER

The winning sportsmen take the crown
And losers never know renown.
Let's honour the unfortunate,
The awkward, slow, and second-rate.

The marathon aspirant who,
While racing from St. Paul's to Kew,
Mistook his way and last was seen
Between Carlisle and Gretna Green.
A cheer for him, my friends, a cheer for him.

The putter circling with his shot.
Resolved to give it all he's got,
Who conjured up a mighty throw
But then forgot to let it go.
A cheer for him, my friends, a cheer for him.

The channel swimmer keeping trim
By going on a sponsored swim,
Who tried to cross the Upper Nile
But met a hungry crocodile.
A cheer for him, my friends, a cheer for him.

The walker, finishing so late
The race from York to Harrogate,
Who found he'd missed the final train
And had to walk back home again.
A cheer for him, my friends, a cheer for him.

The tosser, looking slim and slight,
Who ran with caber held upright,
Then found his strength begin to go
And dropped it on the umpire's toe.
A cheer for him, my friends, a cheer for him.

The fencer with a technique flawed
Rehearsing movements with his sword,
Who cried, "On guard!" took up the pose
And amputated half his nose.
A cheer for him, my friends, a cheer for him

The runner with the killing pace
Who won the London-Brighton race
And fell exhausted, glassy-eyed
Then found he'd been disqualified.
A cheer for him, my friends, a cheer for him

The wrestler tangling with his foe
Who seized an unresisting toe
And sank his teeth in to the bone
But found he'd bitten through his own.
A cheer for him, my friends, a cheer for him.

So though the winners take the crown
And losers never know renown,
Remember the unfortunate,
The awkward and the second rate.
A cheer for them, my friends, a cheer for them.

BUSINESS AS USUAL DURING ALTERATIONS

DO COME TO CHURCH the notice cried;
YOUR TRANSPORT NEEDS PROVIDED FOR.
How kind, I thought, but then I spied
A builder's skip beside the door.

FAIR'S FAIR

Old Blue, the chow
Inspired this verse
When in his mouth
 I saw a purse;
For by his side
There strode old Joan
Whose teeth held tight
A mutton bone.

ATLANTIC FLIGHT

Across the ocean Lindbergh flew,
His plane the water skimming;
He went by air (as friends all knew)
Because he hated swimming.

LAMENT FROM A STATELY HOME

The guv'nor had some fun
Way back in nineteen-one;
He shot a score of bear among the ice-caps.
He stuffed 'em, large and small,
Stood two up in the hall
And sold the rest for quite a pretty price, chaps.

In '13 on the Nile
He was hunting crocodile
On a raft, with just his rifle and some guide-maps;
He shot one in the ear,
When its mate attacked his rear,
And had his bags and all the bits inside, chaps.

He stayed in '24
With Chumley in Lahore
And they tried to catch a tiger in their cat-traps;
Well, one fell in of course
So did Chumley and his horse
Though they only found his stirrups and his hat, chaps.

And then in '52
He went hunting caribou
(Though we told him that he ought to have a rest, p'raps); He
bagged a handsome pair –
Then he met a grizzly bear –
And we buried what was left of him out West, chaps.

All that was long ago.
And now, with funds so low,
We only shoot at woodcock, snipe and grouse, chaps;
And if our cash runs out
For our sport without a doubt
We'll down to putting cheeses into mouse-traps.

NOISE

I've catalogued sounds that may often displease;
There's the scraping of fiddles, the singing of glees,
The wailing of ghosts as they jangle their keys,
The roaring of waves in tempestuous seas,
The whining of gnats when you're taking your ease.
The screaming of jets and a violent sneeze,
The gurgling of victims of cut-throat thuggees.
The screeching of brakes and a gale through the trees,
The buzzing of bluebottles, hornets and bees,
The bellow of bulls as you walk through the leas;
But much more distressing than any of these
Is the publican's, "Time, all you gentlemen, please!"

MENDEL NEVER THOUGHT OF THIS

My book says that Hannibal crossed the Alps with elephants.
Historically that seems to be an irrelevance.
Biologically it's interesting – if indeed it' s fact –
But it sounds to me as if the author is a wee bit cracked.

*****

Take a male kangaroo
(A tame one will do),
Let it mate with a mink
And – unless she should block it –
You will get, I should think,
A fur coat with a pocket.

HE

He has a name
He has a head
His blood and flesh
Are used as bread

He has a house
He has a land
No man his peace
Can understand

He has a voice
He has a word
And of himself
He's but a third

He has no sire
He has no dam
But speaks his name
I Am, I Am

He has his brides
He has his day
He knows no night
And nor do they

The once He died
But straight uprose
Though where He is
God only knows

TEST MATCH SPECIAL

They talk of this, they talk of that.
The commentators chew and chat
On Boris Karloff (William Pratt),
The Mayor of Toytown, Postman Pat
And even Jacques Delors;
They talk about the umpire's hat,
The habits of the horseshoe bat,
The college C.M.J was at,
The kangaroos in Ballarat –
But they never give the score.

They talk of Caesar's book on Gaul,
A pigeon wooing on the wall.
The early letters of St. Paul,
And nights in Bangalore;
They talk of Voce and Gladstone Small,
Slackhampton's annual Cricket Ball,
A listener's postcard, Hadrian's Wall,
In fact – of anything at all –
Except, of course, the score.

They talk of Gatting's appetite.
Spectators on a building site.
They tell of games at Piddlebright,
What Aggers did on Friday night
And Dorothy Lamour;
They talk of cakes, potato blight,
The physics of a ball in flight.
The hymns of Henry Francis Lyte
And Jonadab the Rechabite, –
But they never give the score.

But when a streaker all aglow
(I think this one was Fulham Flo)
Disturbed one day the status quo
By racing on the pitch to show
Her charms behind, before, –
Did they describe her top and toe
(And elsewhere that was apropos)
Or even mention her? Oh, no!
They read the score-card (very slow)
A dozen times or more.

WEDDING NIGHT

An innocent bridegroom, named Paul,
Of sex had no knowledge at all;
When his bride said, "I'm nude,
Now do something rude."
He got up and wrote BUM on the wall.

RUMINATIONS ON ELEPHANTS

Everybody who has been to the zoo has an inkling
That the elephant's skin is subject to wrinkling;
But not everybody knows why this is rife –
Not even the elephant or his wife.
If you go to zoologist for an answer
(And you might as well go to a belly-dancer)
He is bound to propound the standard theory
(And it is one I queory)
That the wrinkles act as channels for mud
And that they have done this efficiently since the time of the
            Flood.
But, as an explanation, this is far too glib,
And probably a fib.

I shall offer my reasons for this phenomenon and you shall sit
            in judgement.
And, if you disagree, I shall bear you no grudgement.
No elephant has had his skin tailored
And, if it had been, then the cutters ought to be jailored. Their
            skins always come off the pegs
And elephants are notorious for having awkward inside legs.
In some cases the elephant's body has shrunk,
Even its trunk.
And the skin becomes flabbier
And sometimes shabbier.

For far too long in the water elephants will often linger
And then they contract their equivalent of washerwoman's
        finger.
They have large mouths and a good sense of humour and,
        sequently
They tend to guffaw frequently.
When they laugh they don't just shake
They quake.
But laughter is a great wrinkler
Particularly if it is the belly variety and not just a tinkler.
And, as the wrinkles form, the elephants immediately start
        ruing it
Because there is so much of them doing it.
Then they worry and that causes more wrinkles
And, even in severe cases, krinkles.

So, you see, when dealing with the skin of elephants, be they
        Africans or Asians
Scientists do not have a monopoly of theories on their
        undulations.
And perhaps my ideas on these Probisideans
Will overthrow those of the zoologists as Gideon overthrew
the Midians.

Finally, I would like to say that all is not lost;
At very little cost
The wrinkling may be rectified by ironing
Which would quickly smooth out the elephants environing
But, where this is not practicable, I would recommend in all
          other cases
That the skin be tightened by fitting elephants with suspenders
          and braces.

YOU CAN'T ANSWER THAT

He said he was a gentleman
And could prove it, what was more;
He showed me where he worked and it
Was written on the door.

BEHOLD THE BIRDS OF THE AIR: THEY SOW NOT NOR REAP – BUT THEY'VE GOT ONE OR TWO OTHER TRICKS UP THEIR PLUMAGE

The vicar's daughter came to tea
When I was still a lad;
A prunes-and-prisms spinster she,
Her age some forty-two or three,
Her name Griselda Gadd.

When tea was cleared, I went outside
To see the swifts in flight;
I'd often stand there saucer-eyed
And watch them wheel and dart and glide
From height to giddy height.

That night, Miss Gadd came out to share
The acrobatic show;
I told her swifts were very rare.
They fed and slept while in the air.
And never came to woe.

She smiled and said, "All feathered things
Are made by God above;
He fashioned every one that sings,
And gave them, all their tiny wings
To show that He is love."

I told her that they mate in flight
And illustrated how;
I said, it's such a super sight,
And – oh, Miss Gadd – up on the right,
A pair are at it now."

Griselda Gadd was horrified,
Her face a ketchup red;
She quickly turned to go inside
And as she went with solid stride,
"Disgusting boy!" she said.

IT'S A CONSPIRACY

It seems that the older I get
The harder they're making the chairs,
The stiffer the doors and the lower the floors
Not to mention the steeper the stairs.

GUARDIAN ANGELS

Mark and Matthew, Luke and John
Guard the bed that I lie on;
But while I'm having it away
You needn't feel obliged to stay.

FOR THE TWENTY-FIRST CENTURY
NURSERY

Mary, Mary, (contemporary)
How does your garden grow?
I've poppies white
And hops upright
And cannabis all in a row.

*

Jack Spratt would eat no fat
And lean caused her disquiet.
He abhorred cholesterol
And she was on a diet.

*

Georgy-Porgy, pudding and pie
Kissed the boys and made them cry;
When the girls came out to play –
Georgy-Porgy ran away.

*

There was an old woman
Who lived in a shoe;
She didn't have children –
She knew what to do.

Humpty-Dumpty went to the wall.
Aerosol paint and spray-gun withal.
But the resources
Of all the Mayor's men
Couldn't erase the graffiti again.

*

Polly put the telly on
Polly put the telly on
Polly put the telly on
And we'll watch Nationwide.

Sukey switch it off again
Sukey switch it off again
Sukey switch it off again
The detector van's outside.

MISSION IMPOSSIBLE

The Lord said, "Love thy neighbour,"
And I hope he's well aware
That to that end I'd labour –

But her husband's always there.

NOW IT CAN BE TOLD

We three kings from orient were.
Kings from eastern lands afar,
Caspar, Melchior, Balthazar,
Followed long that guiding star
The holy child to see.
Eyes upcast, they rode arow
Staring at that star aglow
Till at last they sank below
The waves of Galilee.

*****

The Ark was full, secure the door.
The rain swamped pit and peak;
The rising flood the Ark upbore
But soon, alas, not anymore;
The water filtered through the floor.
"O close the heavens, Lord," said Noah,
"We've sprung a bloody leak!"

*****

I'll make this water wine for thee
According to thy wishes.
I give the mystic sign – and see
The trans forma— oh, silly me
It's come out loaves and fishes.

*****

The tribes at Sinai Moses eyed
And found him empty handed.
"But where's the Decalogue?" they cried.
He bit his lip and then replied,
"I've lost them to be candid."

*****

With sling and pebble David came
To keep the fateful tryst.
He faced Goliath, took his aim.
Released the stone and blushed for shame.
"Oh, dear," he said, "I've missed!"

*****

"No harm would ever come to thee
From eating apples red,"
The snake insisted 'neath the tree;
But Eve would not thus tempted be;
"You bugger off," she said.

*****

The widow cried, "My son is dead!"
Her face was wan and wizen.
Elijah took the lad to bed
Where on him thrice his body spread –
And found himself in prison.

RIPOSTE

(from a modern poet to a critic)

My Vegan Gavotte
You depicted as rot
And you set out your wherefore and why;
Though you haven't a clue
You've a right to your view
But I must make the point – so have I!

Of course there's no rhyme.
But that's not a crime!
And, besides, 1 don't have to comply
With the old fashioned rules
That are followed by fools –
For a modernist poet am I!

You say there's no stress
And my rhythm's a mess.
They are charges I shall not deny;
But metre's old hat –
You ought to know that –
And we're better without it, say I!

I can see you're confused
By the words that I've used;
I invented them, as you imply.
But I often do that –
All the rest are so flat
Whereas mine show the innermost I!
The conventions I scorn!
My Gavotte is the dawn
Of the day when no rules shall apply!
Now you said as you panned it
You don't understand it;
Well, – candidly, mate, neither do I!

IT'S BEING SO CHEERFUL AS KEEPS ME GOING

So you've arrived at last…
Well, that clock's slow, not fast!
I know you've flown here from Bangkok,
But visits start at three o'clock
And now it's twenty past.

I've been a week in here;
It seems more like a year.
There's too much noise to read or write,
The television bores me tight
And headphones hurt my ear.

You've grapefruit there I see.
Well that's no good to me.
I only eat them if they're tinned
And even then they give me wind
From breakfast round to tea.

There's no-one visits me, –
Not friends nor family;
Well, only just to say, 'Hello…
How are you now… We'll have to go…
There's someone else to see.''

This place has gone to pot;
The staff don't give a jot.
They bring your meals and make your bed.
They check if you're alive or dead.
And that's about your lot.

I told the senior nurse
Since being here I'm worse.
I'm feeling colder every day
And stiffer too, but all she'll say,
"Is do you want a hearse?"

Whenever I complain
That I can't sleep for pain
They keep my pills back far too long
And then they get the dosage wrong
So I can't wake again.

The food they serve is vile;
The soups are more like bile.
The cocoa's stewed, the coffee's weak.
The meat's a case of hide and seek
And tastes of crocodile.

The paper's always late.
The porters call me mate.
The chaplain drinks the patients' beer;
We don't have proper fish in here
We only get the bait.

The sister's speech is slurred…
They've gone! … Well that's absurd!
I didn't see the buggers go;
Still – why they came I'll never know –
They didn't say a word.

BOOT HILL

Here beneath this bank
Lies Sheriff Henry Meecher
Killed when Cock-eyed Frank
Tried to shoot the preacher.

Also by this bank
Lies Preacher Amos Kelf
Killed when Cock-eyed Frank
Tried to shoot himself.

*****

The fastest gunman in the West
Is buried in this plot
But Doc McGovern says he's jest
As dead as those he shot.

*****

Here lie the remains of Tumbleweed Oddie,
His vile career now ended;
He died when he found more holes in his body
Than ever God intended.

*****

Here lies the body of Hank McNair
A rustler from Tuscaloos
Who tried to dance on air
While his neck was in a noose.

*****

The Dalton Brothers' favourite prank
(The preacher called it a sin)
Was taking money from a bank
Before they'd paid it in.

But the banks had something up their sleeves
(Their staff were merry folk);
They made believe the boys were thieves
And shot them for a joke.

*****

Here lies Nevada Ned
Poisoned by lead.

DEBRETT

See prince and peer and paladin,
The rank and arms, the seat and birth;
The cast-list of the actors in
The longest running farce on earth.

THE JOBS NOT FOR ME, MA'AM
(THOUGH I WOULDN'T MIND THE SACK)

(On learning that my name had been included on a list
forwarded to the Queen for consideration for the Poet
Laureateship)

For your personal bard, Ma'am
My name disregard, Ma'am;
If I were selected you'd rue it;
For if truth I'm a cad –
More depraved than my dad
(Though how happy he was when he knew it).

I know I've the knack
And I'm partial to sack
But I'm amorous after a few. Ma'am;
Then there's safety for no-one,
Be they high or a low one –
From your junior housemaid to you, Ma'am.

I write about vicars
Just to rhyme them with knickers
(As ribaldry that's just for starters)
And now and again
About dirty old men
And their fetish for corsets and garters.

I cavort in the nude
(I was lewder in Bude)
And I say things you'd think were obscene;
I've written on walls
From St. Just to St. Paul's
And I've made a rude noise at the Dean.

I revel at nights
In satanical rites
With familiars, fiends and carousers;
My tail (very narrow)
Is tipped like an arrow
And tucked down the leg of my trousers.

My diet is spare –
Vegetarian fare;
Pimientos, brazil-nuts and Force;
But since I caught rabies
I breakfast on babies
(With mermaids on Fridays of course).

Seduction's the name
 Of my favourite game
And on poets I practise my spell;
If they're torpid or staid
Well, I'm never dismayed –
Poetesses will do just as well.

So please let it be
Any poet but me –
I shouldn't be piqued in the least. Ma'am;
And I don't have the time
For much dabbling in rhyme –
I've enough on my plate as a priest, Ma'am.

VARIATIONS ON A THEME

(My grandmother's remedy of counting sheep to induce
slumber has no rival in my experience. From 'Mrs. Grimes'
Household Hints)

Insomniacs in general
Will tally ovine hosts
But I'm a vegetarian
And favour nutty roasts.

*****

When counting sheep
To foster sleep
Include both ewe and tup;
If still awake
At morning break
I think you'd best get up

*****

While shepherds watched their flocks by night
Upon the mountain steep,
One counted up to ninety-nine
And slithered into sleep.

*****

Last night I floated into slumber
Counting sheep of endless number;
My wife's repose was frail and fleeting.
Ruined by persistent bleating.

*****

The canny sheep
Who cannot sleep
Will count up leaping shepherds;
But slumber shuns
The stupid ones
Who think of sheeping leopards.

BRIEF CASE

Try basting your turkey with port -
Use anything up to a quart.
With stout in the pud
Some rum would be good –
Then life will be merry, but short.

THE SIX WIVES OF HENRY VIII
CLERIHEWED

Catharine of Aragon
A virtual paragon
Objected when Henry began to sin
With Anne Boleyn.

Anne Boleyn
Consorted carnally with her kin;
But she caused the most annoy
Performing encores with the hoi-polloi.

Jane Seymour
 Didn't know there'd be three more;
She went bedward, sighed,
Produced Edward and died.

Anne of Cleves
Might as well have been Jeeves
For all that happened after she was wed
In bed.

Catharine Howard
Was never a coward
Given Henry's notoriety –
And hers for impropriety.

Catharine Parr
Shouted, "Hurrah
Six times he wived
And I survived!"

DEATH OF A BAR-FLY

A foot was planted on the rail.
An elbow on the bar;
They said he held the counter up -
It really looked bizarre.

They said he'd been there fifty years –
A publican's delight;
The earliest patrons found him there,
The last ones said, "Good-night."

They said he died there at his post
And left a glass of brown;
They had to prise his limbs away –
And then – the bar fell down.

EVERY TIME UPON A TIME

I wonder why the would-be bard
Accepts it as the norm
That stories told in verse require
The use of ballad form.

What's wrong, I would ask, with the tercet?
I know there are some who would curse it.
But it's fun (though one needs to rehearse it).

Or blank verse, agent of the Stratford Bard
Who deemed it (as did Boris) good enough.

There are so many different forms you will find
When you're deep in the subject immersed;
For example sestets (which of course are six-lined):
As to rhyming there's no regulation to bind
And the feet may be any for which you've a mind
(These are anapests – dactyls reversed).

Then there's the haiku
But, if you hate foreign stuff,
Try the limerick –

Anapestic, attractive and fecund.
There are only two rhymes it is reckoned;
The fourth with the third
And from that you've inferred
It's the fifth with the first and the second.

Work in hexameters sometimes, though editors tend to dislike them
Dactyls, and five as a rule, with a trochee or spondee to follow
(Longfellow's poem 'Evangeline' offers a perfect example).

Other forms there are, like the quinzaine, epode,
Sonnet, rondel, dithyramb, Greater Sapphics
(Not to be confused with the Lesser form unfolding before you),

and vers libre, with a little alliteration
prosody precepts repudiating
option puffball soft
but ballad-form Gilpin-renowned
wedding guest wiser
pre-
pollent –

which-goes-of-course-di-da-di-da,
Di-da-di-da-di-da,
I-am bus-es-ad-nause-am,
Di-da-di-bloo-di-da!

NO FLOWERS PLEASE

A half-stifled cough
Made me look up

An elderly clergyman
Wondered what I was doing

I wasn't surprised
Or offended
After all
It isn't every day
One sees a sober-suited
Middle-aged gentleman
Solemnly pouring a pint of Guinness
Over a grave
In an obscure village churchyard

She was my auntie
I told him
She hated fuss and flowers
But loved a glass of Guinness
Or two

He mused a moment
Then shook his head
Sadly I thought
He said
And she is elsewhere now you know

She'd have appreciated it
I smiled
Side-stepping the implied reproach
But I've paid my respects
And I must go

He walked a little way with me
Still troubled about propriety I think
Though he didn't pursue it

In fact
He said nothing more at all except
Oh my goodness
When a sharp report behind us
Broke into the evening stillness
Of that obscure village churchyard

It was a brief but unmistakable burp.

HOLD THAT POSE

I wish I could see the reaction
(It's a picture no artist has drawn)
Of an adder that bites on a nettle
Or a wasp as it sits on a thorn.

AGATHA CHRISTIE! THOU SHOULD'ST BE LIVING AT THIS HOUR.

(News item: – The police are hoping to interview a man observed near the scene of the crime. He was middle-aged, of average build and of medium height.)

"I heard it, sergeant, on the news –
There's been a murder in The Mews.
It said a body had been found
On Friday evening, gagged and bound;
And Scotland Yard are very keen
To interview a person seen
Proceeding from the passage-way
Near where the victim's body lay.

Apparently he's male and white.
Of average build and medium height;
He could be fifty – maybe less
And probably in normal dress…
Well, that description, as you see,
Uncannily resembles me!
So take me in, though I admit
I don't remember doing it."

"I'll do that, sir," said Sergeant Slee,
And thank you for your honesty.
The case, though, we thought quickly solved
Becomes each day the more involved.
Our profile fits so many males
We've prisoners for twenty jails.
We're holding here alone – let's see...
Including you now, thirty-three."
But when he put him in the cell
He paused - then went inside as well.
"I ought," he said, "to be with you –
That chap's description fits me too.
Besides, unless I tell a lie
1 can't produce an alibi...
Here, constable, please lock the door
And call me number thirty-four!

And – make room lads, for just one more."

THE POWER OF PRAYER

The patient cried, "Oh, God, please help!
The pain is more than I can bear!"
A moment's silence, then she belched;
And with a changed, more tranquil air.
She said," I feel much better now."

How wonderful the power of prayer!

TALES OF A FISHWIFE

THE SAD CASE OF THE MYOPIC OCTOPOD

A short-sighted octopus seeking a bride
Couldn't make out the belles from the hag-types;
He sobbed and he sighed and he finally died
In attempting to mate with some bagpipes.

THE JELLYFISH

Although the strong-belly-fish
Enjoy eating shelly-fish
They make the poor jelly-fish
A trifle unwelly-ish.

FAINT PRAISE

I like the chub
But not as grub.

WHAT'S THE MATTER WITH YOU?

The plaice has blotches on his back
His features show surprise.
He's just found out he's suffering
From spots behind his eyes.

HOLY, HOLY, HOLY

The saithe is from exclusive stock
And not the common horde;
His name goes back to Bible times -
They call him Saithe the Lord.

THE DORY

The dory's a very slow mover.
But he never goes hungry for prey;
He uses his mouth like a hoover
And it's sucked in from miles away.

HE'S NO RELATION OF MINE

The freshwater burbot
Is unlike the turbot.
The turbot's a flat fish
And looks rather odd;
The burbot's a fat fish
And kin to the cod.

ELEGY WRITTEN AFTER VISITING A
STATELY HOME

A stately home of fifty-seven rooms,
With maids and butlers, gardeners and grooms,
A thousand acres, forest, lake and farms,
A second home (a manor-house in Kent),
A title and a seat in Parliament.

"But how was this acquired?" I asked the guide.
'The lord was heir to it," the man replied.
"The first Earl fell while fighting for his queen
And she rewarded him with this demesne."

Now I had fallen too, but my rewards
Were not as splendid as the ancient lord's.
I had (the earth was never for the weak) –
A letter, badge and five pounds odd a week –
A pension yearly re-assessed and sheared
Until it altogether disappeared.

But why exists this wide disparity
Between the Earl and (ex-lance-corporal) me?
We served our queens alike, we fought and bled –
It must have been some little thing I said.

CAD

Within the pushchair sat a lad
Who, as he passed me, gurgled, "Dad!"

And though I said, "Hello!" and smiled.
Of course 1 hadn't sired the child.

But then I saw his mother there
Bewitching, dainty, debonair,

And I confess I felt a cad –
I wished - oh, how I wished I had!

I turned about as she went by
And watched her with a lustful eye

But walking backwards still in thrall
Tumbled over someone's wall.

ON THE DOLE

My arteries are in a mess
The x-rays show it;
I'm told I must avoid all stress –
And me – a poet!

AY, THERE'S THE RUB.

Do sardines dream of tins
And pigs of Sunday roast?
Do winkles dream of pins
And anchovies of toast?

Do turtles dream of soups
And common eels of jelly?
And turkeys in their coops
Of adverts on the telly?

Do lobsters dream of pots
Or flies of swats and sprays?
And oats of brawny Scots
And whales of ladies' stays?

Do bullocks dream of mustard
And cauliflowers of cheese?
Does rhubarb dream of custard
And cod of chips and peas?

I'LL READ THE MAPS – YOU DRIVE

Our car is driven by my wife
And I've been the map-reader all our married life.
I do it exceptionally well.
This is easy to tell
Since we always arrive at our destinations
Safely and without complications.
Mistakes do not occur when I am in the maps immersed
But I can't understand why my wife needs to study them first

FAITH AND BELT AND BRACES

The plaque in the porch said, "We trust in the Lord.
This church was erected in faith by his people."
But its doors were kept locked, it was fully insured
And a lightning conductor surmounted the steeple.

CHILDREN

They delight so
At weanage
Not quite so
At teenage.

TO A WORDSWORTH

O Lakeland bard, I honour thee,
But for the very life of me
I know not why thou should'st rejoice
To hear the vagrant cuckoo's voice.

Thou goest o'er the top, old thing,
To call it 'darling of the spring;'
Its double-noted mating call
Is quite the dullest of them all.

"O blessèd bird," thou dost indite.
In truth it is a parasite
Equippèd with a faculty
For shameless self-publicity.

Thy rapture one might understand
If, lying on some silvery strand,
Or, musing in a shady nook,
Thou heard it sing just once oocuck.

Thou'd not have won thy wide renown
(still less the Laureate's glorious crown)
If thou'd expressed thyself in rhyme
With Wordsworth, Wordsworth all the time.

KISS OF LIFE

The youth adored the pretty nurse;
But, as she could not be his wife,
He threw himself beneath her horse
To win at least the kiss of life.

He heard her run to where he lay.
Inert, but restless for the bliss.
She knelt beside him first to pray
And then – the long awaited kiss.

The breath that passed their lips between
Was like a rancid garlic sauce;
The fickle youth then wished he'd been
Resuscitated by the horse!

IRRITATION

An angry mother kangaroo
Chastising joey roughly said,
"No matter what your friends all do,
I'll not you have crisps in bed."

THE JOKER

The young religious zealot was
On my conversion bent;
He tried for half an hour or more –
But lost the argument.

Then I, by way of jesting, said,
"My friend, you ought to know
You waste your time, for I adore
The gods of long ago.

I worship Zeus, the father-god,
Apollo, Artemis,
Poseidon, Dionysus, Ops,
Persephone and Dis,"

My caller stood there goggle-eyed;
He'd never heard such names
And asked if he could bring along
A deacon, Brother James.

I didn't mind, so later on
He brought him to my door.
I listed all the gods again
And added several more.

The deacon listened, open-mouthed,
And stood like one in shock;
Then asked if I'd consent to meet
An Elder of the flock.

My hoax was giving me such fun
I readily agreed,
And when he came, I praised my gods
And sang a spurious creed.

That brought an invitation from
The chairman, Brother Birch,
For me to talk about my gods
To members at his church.

I shook with inward mirth and I
Consented to attend.
I thought how droll all this would seem
To my agnostic friend.

I made my speech the Sunday next
The audience was rapt.
I spoke an hour and at the end
They stood and cheered and clapped.

I'd listed all the deities
Whose names occurred to me;
Their duties, their relationships
And each one's history.

"The fear of many gods," I said,
"I must, my friends, dispel.
Once you discover who does what –
The system functions well.

The Grecian gods are specialists;
It's each one to his call.
The tasks are skimped in other schemes
Where one performs them, all."

That night they tossed their god aside;
His duties hence would cease.
In future they would idolize
The gods of Ancient Greece.

The church is now a temple where
They worship, pray and feast.
It's called The Sacred Pantheon
And I've been made the priest!

But I'm not gratifying now
My penchant for a jest;
The gods I saw afresh that night.
My views I re-assessed.

The points I'd made were powerful;
They seemed to cast a spell.
Indeed, so strong they proved, that I
Convinced myself as well!

ROYAL COUSINS

(Question from a recent examination paper; Outline the causes
of the antipathy between Elizabeth and Mary Queen of Scots.)

Mary was a Scot;
Bess was not.

Bess was a Prot;
Mary was not.

Mary begot;
Bess did not.

THEY'VE GOT A CARD FOR THAT

If you get married or retire,
Adopt a dog or cat,
Indite a greeting or expire –
They've got a card for that.

You're made a granddad – such a thrill –
You throw aloft your hat;
It's naught to do with you, but still
There is a card for that.

There isn't one for standing bold
On Ilkley Moor 'baht 'at
But if you catch your death from cold
They've got a card for that.

When moving to a home that's new
There's one for that as well.
Though 'Bless This House' will hardly do
When home's a prison cell.

You catch a fish – the first you win –
And, though it' s just a sprat –
And one before it pulled you in –
There'll be a card for that.

You fail your driving-test, alack!
But there's a card for you;
Your tester has a heart-attack –
There's one for widows, too.

They've cards for people always late
Through living hurly-burly;
And one for those who cannot wait
And send their greetings early.

For babies new to mother's knee
A 'Welcome' card is vended,
With space to add 'Especially
If that's what you intended.'

If you don't speak to those below
Or in the upstairs flat.
They've got a card that's blank, and so
There's even one for that.

If people think that you are dead
The cards are edged with black;
But if you rise up from your bed
They come and take them back!

PUSES, PI OR PODS?

I love to see an octopus
That's swimming; in the wild;
My pleasure is enhanced because
I know how it is styled.

It's when it gathers with its friends
I tend towards nonplus;
The truth is I do not know
The plural octopus.

I've heard of octopuses and
I've heard of octopi,
Octopodes and octopods.
But which is right – and why?

I don't mind seeing, when alone,
A shoal of them together;
But, if I'm with a friend, well then
I talk about the weather.

EPIGRAM ON AN INTELLECTUALLY
CHALLENGED WOMAN

When asked if he'd look at her brain
The surgeon responded, "Oh, blimey!
It's going to be such a strain –
I don't have a microscope by me!"

GETTING AWAY FROM IT ALL

It causes city men to grieve
When they're by urban smells confined,
So some will seek the Broads and leave
Polluted air behind.

They claim that for their brief reprieve
The motor-boat was well designed;
They have their break, go home and leave
Polluted Broads behind.

THE FARMER'S BOY

(What really happened)

The sun went down behind the hill
Across the dreary moor,
When, weary and lame,
A boy there came
Unto the farmer's door;
"Can you tell me
If any there be
Who will give me employ?
To plough and sow
To reap and mow
And be a farmer's boy?"

The farmer's wife said, "Husband dear
This lad is sore distressed;
Oh give him bread
And let his head
Upon my bosom rest.
And by and by
He'll taste my pie
And many other joy,
And you shall sow
And daughter mow
And I'll support the boy."

The daughter whispered, "Father, dear
Your ear to him incline;
Oh, bid him stay.
And take, I pray.
The bedroom next to mine;
For in the Mead
I sore have need
For such a lusty boy;
And while you sow
And Ma does mow
I'll give him such employ!"

The farmer cried,
"I'll hear no more!
He'll not with me abide.
He'll take my croft
When I'm aloft,
My daughter for his bride.
No balladeers
Adown the years
Of me will sing and scoff.
I'll plough alone
And die unknown –
So he can bugger of!"

MURDER AT THE PARISH PARTY

My black ace made me the murderer
So I had to feign to strangle
Anyone I could trace in the gloom

But what I clutched
When the time came
Was too soft for a neck

I tried again
And again
But only my fourth desperate squeeze
Provoked a cry

Not a scream as required by the rules
But a cry of considerable pain

The awful truth was suddenly only too plain
My victim was standing on something
A foot from the floor
And it wasn't her neck I'd been squeezing

I struck nothing in my flight for anonymity
And when the light was switched on
I was far from the buxom Miss Blaine
Anguished and angry

I wasn't unmasked as the culprit
Nor shamed as a molester
And I didn't confess
In fact
The detective accused the Curate
And he
For no apparent reason
Except perhaps that nobody else owned up
And it was all very embarrassing
Proclaimed his guilt
And could we play the game again

SURPRISE, SURPRISE

Some horses run faster than others
It's a fact that one cannot disguise.
Then why on the televised racing
Should broadcasters show such surprise?

KINSHIP

Zebras aren't related to llamas.
They're donkeys in striped pyjamas.

ALL ABOARD FOR SIRIUS

Outstretched before a blazing fire
A sleepy spaniel's dreams aspire
Towards the canine heaven, which lies
Within the dog-star in the skies;
Where breeds of every height and girth
May bay unchecked at moon and earth.

He sees an endless heavenly street
With lamp-posts every twenty feet
And stretching far till distance dims,
With baggy trousers, juicy limbs.
Fat postmen, blind to twitching paws.
Excited eyes and slavering jaws.

He dreams he sniffs eternally
At odours in variety.
Imagines cats that never die,
Of chasing them across the sky,
Of fires to stare at, doors to claw,
Old shoes to chew and bones to gnaw.

In heaven there are no guns, no snares,
No hunts, no artificial hares;
No barbers' shops, no ladies' laps.
No Crufts, no kennels, chains or straps;
No sheep, no barges, sleds or war,
No night work with Securicor.

But then he wakes and looks around;
But only sees terrestrial ground –
His basket, rug and dinner-plate.
His collar, leash and chain – but wait! –
Are these unreal? It isn't plain.
He thinks he'll go to sleep again.

AT THE CHRISTENING

The clergy-man sprinkled the baby with water
And proudly the parents regarded their daughter;
She looked up and smiled in the clergyman's face
From his arms, where she lay in her satin and lace.
And she burbled and blushed as he named her Simone
Then conducted a christening rite of her own.

CIRCUMGYRATIONS

The earth circumvolves on its axis
Diurnally (once every day);
A bias (or bent)
That by common consent
Is a highly commendable trait.

And as daily it turns on its axis
So yearly it circles the Sunne;
(That's archaic, I know it, –
But being a poet
I thought I would spell it like Donne.)

And the system itself is revolving –
Around what I don't know, I admit
(I was never omniscient)
But I've written sufficient
To support my contention, to wit:–

That, because of these circumgyrations.
It's really no wonder at all
That one's brain is a Babel
And legs so unstable
That often we falter and fall.

This concept to me is as simple
As that dawn to the day must surrender;
My wife though, I fear.
Cannot grasp the idea
(I suspect it's to do with her gender).

But she'll always return to the subject
(With the oddest of looks in her eye)
When I've been to the Ham
Or the Marquis of Kara
Though I'm damned if I understand why.

DON'T MOVE – I'VE GOT YOU DISCOVERED – OR I WILL HAVE WHEN I'VE FOUND MY GLASSES

Had my sight
In the light
Been as keen
As my hark
In the dark
You'd have been
O mosquito
Finito

THE FINAL WORD

An autocrat was Clare,
A wimp her husband Tim;
And everyone was well aware
She dominated him.

But how complete her sway.
How feeble he could be,
I never knew until the day
They dined at home with me.

When bidding them adieu,
The evening being spent.
Abruptly Clare said, "Tim – the loo!"
And like a child, he went.

When next I met with Tim
I thought I'd le t him know
Just how I sympathised with him.
That Clare abused him so.

He grinned. "It sounds absurd.
Old fellow, but it's true –
I always have the final word!"
"But, Tim," I cried, – "The loo!"

"Oh I got back at Clare,"
He said and grinned again.
"I didn't do a thing in there, –
I only pulled the chain!"

SO...?

Christmas comes but once a year
People often say.
But now I come to think of it
So does every day.

OK YOUR MARK...

"I'll run away," cried Mrs. Bird,
"To Mother down at Bristol!"
Her husband uttered not a word
But fired a starting pistol.

P's FOR PREDATORS

There's peppered soil above my peas
But all the cats ignore it;
And though they doubtless cough and sneeze
They sniff, they scratch and bore it.

Voracious mice invade the site
From gardens quite remote;
They eat the upturned peas despite
Their coats of creosote.

Surviving seeds then swell and sprout
But first to show are fated;
They're spied by sparrows, rooted out
Or roughly amputated.

The rest, though twig-supported, thrive
Then thunder rumbles round
And wind and hail together strive
To beat them to the ground.

The flowers come – and pea-moths too
Yet though I use a spray
Their eggs all hatch and, hid from view.
The maggots munch away.

The jays and pigeons soon detect
The peas that bravely burgeon
And through my nets the pods dissect
As neatly as a surgeon.

Thus ends the annual predation;
My peas are all aheap.
There is, of course, one consolation –
Whatever's left – I keep!

My neighbours' plots I idolize –
Although they both are braggarts;
Their peas will always take a prize
While mine are mostly maggots.

THANKS FOR THE MEMORY

Your youth is fled
Your age confessed
The night your bed
Is used for rest.

GATHER ROUND, BOYS, AND I'LL TELL YOU ABOUT IT

Old Albert, the tenor, was boasting again.
He was pompous, loquacious and terribly vain.
He'd cornered us all and he'd started to trace
His career as a soloist, treble and bass.

His knowledge of musical matters was poor
And we'd heard all his stories so often before.
He'd sung in the choir at his church when a lad
But smoking had ruined such voice as he'd had.

He'd been singing with us for a number of years
And his voice was offensive to everyone's ears.
And though rasping out many an incorrect note
He avowed he could sing all our items by rote.

He was boasting that evening again, as you've read
But he probably spoke with some truth when he said (Though
he wondered why everyone laughed in his face) "I've rendered
'Messiah' all over the place!"

POET'S PROGRESS

When first I wrote, I lived a while
In digs at Bethnal Green;
And had my verse rejected by
The Band of Hope, the Stepney Spy
And Mugsy's Magazine.

But now I have improved my style
I have a flat at Kew;
And daily get rejected by
The Tatler, Lady, Private Eye
And Poetry Review.

I never minded reject slips
From Harper's, Vogue, The Times, Debrett;
But now I've reached an all-time low
With one inscribed, "With love from Flo,
The Nether Stumpington Gazette."

THE MARRIAGE BOND(AGE)

Too late have wedded couples found
Inclining to repentance
That marriage isn't just a word –
It's rather more: a sentence!

NEIGHBOURS

Each time I have purchased a new property
I have always contrived to come a cropperty.
The agents advertise a desirable residence
Fit, they say, for kings or presidents.
That may be true; I have always found my homes desirable,
 But what makes it all so perspirable.
And a matter to deplore.
Are the people next door.

To sell a house, agents will make Herculean labours.
But they never say a thing about the neighbours.
You move in and find there are transistors blaring;
You go into the garden and discover kids all staring.
On one side, there's a dachsund yapping and pretending to greet you
On the other, there's a mastiff slavering and determined to eat you
One neighbour won't stop wittering while you are working.
The other won't stop tittering while you are physical-jerking.
There's one chap with a garden full of weeds
(And before long, your beds will be full of their seeds);
There's another with a garden just like Wisley,
And he sneers at yours and hints that it' s grisly.
He's always burning things and probably suffers from pyromania,
So you spend all the sunny days wishing they were rainier.

All my life, it seems, I've been under a curse
That my neighbours will range from bad to worse. Wherever my plot
I've had the lot;
The roar from the night-out-on-the-towners,
And more from the Knees-up-Mother-Browners;
The irk of the borrow-and-never-pay-backers.
And the smirk from the blow-you-I'm-all-right-Jackers.
The up-with-the Jonses,
The lowering-of-toneses.
The throw-back-our-ballers,
The climb-on-the-wallers.
The scratching of cats.
The squalling of brats.

I often wish I could move in next door so that I could see
What it's like being a neighbour to an inoffensive chap like me.
But I can't do that – it's just an illusion;
I have, however, come to a firm conclusion:
Next time I go in for the house-buying chore,
I'll look for one with desirable residents next door.

PERPETUIM MOBILE

The husband whose wife must be chattering
Till the sweat on her forehead is glistening
Can blame but himself for the battering.
Why doesn't the fathead stop listening?

MY NEW NEIGHBOUR

He studied the seaweed that hung on his wall;
He wetted a finger and raised it.
Releasing a feather, he followed its fall;
He looked at the sky and appraised it.

He walked to a may tree and counted the haws;
His vane he regarded intently.
He mused on a volume of countrymen's saws,
Then fingered his chilblains, but gently.

He asked if I'd seen any snails on the path,
If mosquitoes had gathered at noon;
If a spider had fashioned a web in my bath
Or a nimbus had circled the moon.

I answered his questions with courteous care:
Then he muttered of cock-crow at night.
Of mackerel sky and the tail of a mare.
Of rainbows and shepherds' delight.

He spoke of my roses afflicted with blotch,
And, asked if the stars had been bleared;
He looked at his sundial, adjusted his watch
And, scratching his head, disappeared.

I saw him on telly that very same night –
He'd discarded his seaweed and feather
And, instead, he had charts with a little green light
And was predicting East Anglian weather.

RABBITS AND HARES

Poets use the fact that 'rabbits'
Rhymes conveniently with 'habits'
To sneer at their proclivity
For sexual activity.

Of hares, however, nothing's heard –
There's no suggestive rhyming word.
Though naturalists have always reckoned
That they are similarly fecundF.

THE EARLY BIRD

The bird that early seeks to rise
The proverb says will take the prize.
This worthy habit, I affirm.
Is praised by all – except the worm.

PEASANT LAUGHTER

The wife who lived next door to me
Was busty, brash and massive;
Her husband was the contrary –
Quiescent, puny, passive.

And yet he'd often, late at night.
Guffaw and hoot and jeer.
I thought that this from one so slight
Was curious to hear.

I'd always thought the reason for
The laughter and derision
Was something on the wireless or
A tape or television.

But, no. I passed their house one night
And, looking in, espied
An open fire burning bright
Through curtains drawn aside.

I saw the husband in his chair;
His wife stood by the fire
Undressing and (I had to stare)
Preparing to retire.

I thought that having watched thus far
I'd see what happened after.
Well – she removed her bloated bra
And he collapsed with laughter.

THE MOLE

Moles reside in earthly cavity
Where worms alone can know the gravity
Of all their deeds of dark depravity.
But their degenerate proclivity
The moles pursue in total privity
 For worms are short on perceptivity.

DISILLUSIONMENT

My opinion of man and his creeds
I remember becoming detractory
The day I saw turnips and swedes
Go into a jam-making factory.

DID I SAY SOMETHING?

The cardiographer became
Familiar with my chest
(I'd been despatched to hospital
With cardiac arrest).

I bared it every time she came
And lay down patiently
While she attached the terminals
To take an ECG.

This happened several times a day;
I saw her as a friend.
And felt some sadness when they said
My stay was at an end.

I said goodbye to her beside
The bed on which I'd lain;
And, at that moment, little thought
That we would meet again.

A month or so had passed away
And I thought less of her.
Then, in a crowded shop, I saw
My cardiographer.

I greeted her. She turned about
And smiled uncertainly;
She frowned and it was obvious
She'd quite forgotten me.

I tried to jog her memory –
The conversation hushed.
The other shoppers looked aghast
And as for her – she blushed.

I'm still not sure why this was so;
I only smiled and said
"You'd know me straight away if I
Had nothing on in bed!"

ANTI-SHEEP

Mint
Drops a hint.

SONNET TO SLEEP

(From a room in Papworth Hospital)

Long hours, O Hypnos, have I courted thee
With sacrificial flocks of leaping sheep
To win the blessed boon of dreamless sleep
Which thou uniquely can bestow on me.

I gave thee kings of England, Spain and France,
The stations 'twixt Bexhill and Charing Cross,
The mountain streams in Cromarty and Ross,
The Easter hymns, the Psalms (complete with chants).

And still the gift of slumber thou dost keep
From me, while giving it before the night
To supplicants in rooms to left and right
Who breathe their thanks now stertorous and deep.

Methinks thou lov'st them best beneath the sun
Who, even sleeping, give thee Radio One.

LOGIC

I have noticed of late the affairs of mankind
Are seldom well-ordered and quiet;
A trip to the newsagent's shows they're inclined
To misfortune, disaster and riot.

The headlines on yesterday's papers said GORE,
CATASTROPHE, PANIC and BLOW:
The day before that it was ANGUISH, FURORE,
CALAMITY, SLAUGHTER and WOE.

So, out walking today when I chanced to espy
A poster displayed on a wall
Proclaiming THE END OF THE WORLD DRAWETH NIGH
It didn't surprise me at all.

HARVEST FESTIVAL

Broad beans in the pod
May well come from God
But no-one should view them with lenity;
While all will project
A few are erect
And ought to be thought an obscenity.

SPECTATOR

I couldn't help the guilt feeling
When she left Ken
Friend since scrumping days
But I didn't ask her to
And I couldn't send her back
She said she needed me

I couldn't understand it
I'd never got involved with girls
And hardly knew her anyway

I felt helpless
Watching her move in
Like a spectator

As for Ken
He threatened to kill me
And nearly did on his thousand c.c. bike
Coming like a maniac at me walking
But he turned aside at the last second
As I suppose I might have done
If I'd not been simply spectating.

Her next was an actor
A man of many parts
Like a click and a dialling tone
A sick aunt
An arts class

She took the tensions with her
When she went
Left only one or two puzzled tears behind
But spectators' eyes soon dry

I heard the guy slipped a disc
Before she moved on again
Over-playing the virile lover
I suppose

There was still one thing
Ken and I had to settle
Who was buying the first round

INTIMATIONS OF MORTALITY

Christians knew mortality
In the Coliseum;
Childhood toys have shown it me
In a folk museum.

IT'S HIS AGE YOU KNOW

As a boy I succumbed to the customary brew
Of measles and mumps and an itis or two;
And the doctor, enlisting his knowledge and skill,
Would declare, "It's his age!" and deliver his bill.

My behaviour in youth was imperfect (or worse)
And if I was truculent, pert or perverse
My relations would echo that medical mot
(And especially aunts), "It's his age, don't you know."

They may have been right that my years were to blame.
But now I'm an adult it can't be the same;
Yet my aunts still assert (with the air of a sage)
That the key to my conduct lies still in my age.

When a lady pursued me with love in her eyes
(Or was I the pursuer, the lady the prize?
I'm afraid I've forgotten – my memory is poor)
But my age was the reason – Aunt Fanny was sure.

We married in winter – and parted in spring;
And what else but my age could have caused such a thing?
And when later my passions I sought to revive
That was common, they said, when you've reached thirty-five.

I published a sequence of sonnets on Fate
And achieved some distinction (admittedly late)
But my relations refused to applaud my success;
At forty, they said, they expected no less.

The doctor, who spoke with the mien of the sphinx
Of disorders and age and their mystical links,
Returned to his theme when he diagnosed gout –
"Oh, it's anno and domini – never a doubt!"

I remarried at fifty (my bride was nineteen)
And she wondered if anyone could have foreseen
I'd have chosen a partner so young and so shy.
"My relations," I said, "and they'll soon tell you why!"

I'm sure I shan't know, when I take my last breath,
What a doctor will write as the cause of my death
But if there's a doubt and my aunts get to hear
They'll very soon make it abundantly clear.

***

This postscript is sent from the Heavenly Gate
Where I met with St. Peter ('on being the late').
When I said he looked shrunken he answered me so
"It cometh with age as thou shouldest know."

INVASION AT THE CATHEDRAL

They charge in through the ancient gate;
The quiet close they colonise.
They cry OH! and GEE! and GREAT!
They do not stand and contemplate
But jerk their cameras to their eyes.
They're here, they're there, they're to, they're fro.
They're in, they're out. Ain't this a ball?
Is that the time? O.K. Let's blow!
And through the ancient gate they go,
And see precisely bugger-all.

SUCCESS

My book of verse is out at last
The first edition's selling fast
(Acclaim and cash)

The critics call it very good
They liken me to Thomas Hood
(And Ogden Nash)

Translations published every week
Including Gaelic, Czech and Greek
(And Portuguese)

I win an international prize
I'm recognized in Kensal Rise
(By two Parsees)

I read my verse in Kazakhstan
I'm made the Sultan's right-hand man
(A grand Vizier)

I'm mentioned in the House of Lords
They take my likeness for Tussauds
(I stand with Lear)

I open stores and garden fetes
I'm booked for months with dinner dates
(Champagne and steak)

I'm in the glossy magazines
I'm praised by commoners and queens –
(And then I wake)

MARRIAGE

The prayer-book says N. must take thee
And thou N. when you marry.
That's fine for Neil and Natalie
But not for Flo and Harry.

MEMO TO MY WIFE

I'm well aware, my dearest wife,
You've reached a certain time of life.

You're cold one minute, then you're hot,
And what you wear you'd rather not.

You strip, but just as soon complain,
You've gone from hot to cold again.

But though, my dear, I sympathise,
I wonder if you realise –

When you decide, while we're abed,
As blood upsurges to your head,

The duvet you require no more
And hurl it from you to the floor.

So I from slumber deep awake
With teeth a-chatter, limbs a-shake.

That though my frame may have its flaws –
Yours only has the menopause.

A VERY OLD FAMILY

If there's one thing that gives me the jim-jamilies
It's the claim 'They come from very old families.'
This boasting of ancient lineage,
Where people talk in terms not of pounds and pence but of
        guineage
Is nothing more than vulgar ostentation
Practised by people who wish to shine in the highest
        constellation.
The beginning of all pedigrees
Occurred when our ancestors came down from the trees
Or, depending on what you believe,
With Adam and Eve.

THE GREBE

When grebe-chicks squawk and mother dives
Ostensibly for food,
She's not obeying Nature's drives
But seeking quietude.

ROYAL ENCLOSURE

ARTHUR

King Arthur of Camelot
Would blast and damnelot
His knights, who would interfere
With his consort, Guinevere,
And fill up her pramelot,
 Especially Bedivere
Who acted the ramelot.

RUFUS AND HENRY

I shot an arrow; into the air.
It fell to earth I knew not where;
But, shortly after, Rufus was hearsed
And I was crowned as Henry First.

STEPHEN

Why Stephen of Blois
The Englishmen's Rois
Pursued Matilda
Is puzzling to mois.
Would he have kilda
Or just dishabilda?

KING JOHN

King John, the only--
Lonely and wan –
After losing his baggage in the main
Married again,

FALSE ALARM

King James the Third
Never occurred.

QUEEN VICTORIA

Queen Victoria
Was in a state of euphoria;
John Brown
Was in town.

EDWARD EIGHT

"I'll abdicate;
I've answered 'Yes'
To Mrs. S,"
Said Edward Eight.
"As Baldwin's shirty
The King's regalia
Inter alia
I'll give to Bertie,"

YOU'RE A BETTER MAN THAN MY MUM, GUNGA DIN

In bed my daughter.
She's eight years old;
She wants some water.

I tell her no.
She had her milk
An hour ago.

I hear my daughter.
She's wide awake.
She still wants water.

My temper keep
But sharply say
Be quiet. Sleep.

Again my daughter
She cannot sleep;
She must have water.

Do try to sleep –
The eyelids close
And count up sheep.

Once more my daughter.
She's counted sheep;
She now needs water.

I change my tack.
Just one more sound
She'll get a smack.

A silence now;
At last, contrition.
But no. Not that;
A proposition.

It's when I go
To smack my daughter,
Perhaps I'd take
A glass of water.

ENOUGH SAID

"I now pronounce you man and wife,"
Declared the Reverend Buss.
The couple stayed to hear no more
And said while racing toward the door –
"That's good enough for us!"

DUPLICITY

When of mankind's duplicity I first became aware
I was appalled.
I'd noticed that my barber sold restoratives for hair –
And he was bald.

A healer proved that this was not a lone aberrancy.
He knew no shame
But claimed that cash, his touch and faith could cure infirmity
–
And he was lame.

But, worst of all was Rex, the writer on horoscopy,
Whom I'd admired;
Till hearing that he'd bought a year's supply of stationery
And then expired.

But since I first discovered those depressing human flaws
I've found no other,
Although I've been inclined at times to ask if Santa Claus
Is not my mother.

I'VE GOT RELATIONS IN LOW PLACES

Young Gerry took a little worm
And pierced it with a hook
But as the boy drew back the line
His tail the creature shook.

And said, "One day you'll pay for this;
My kin will square with you.
I've relatives in cemeteries
From here to Timbuctoo"

SAVOYS

To enjoy a Savoy
This method employ
(I verse it – but not like a Byron).
First cut it, de-ice it
But don't slice it or dice it
Till you've pressed all the leaves with an iron.

OTHELLO

(Portrait of a blackbird taken from life. Not painted by T.S.
Eliot.)

Othello is a king; he took possession of my garden
Without so much as by-your-leave or even beg-your-pardon.
A hawthorn is his palace, though he's not there all the time
He has to tour his conquered lands, detect and punish crime.
Receive his subjects' homage, keep insurgent birds at bay
And promulgate his sovereignty a dozen times a day.
And if I should disturb the royal breakfast, lunch or tea
His fearful eye betokens that he thinks to banish me.

Othello is a warrior; he's shrewd and unafraid,
A master of resistance and the swift commando raid.
Disputed borders, worming rights, defence, pre-emptive strike.
To him, no matter what the cause, all combats come alike.
He has a flair for strategy to match his fighting skill
And on every situation he'll impose the royal will;
One moment he'll chastise a thrush who's contravened his law.
The next, against a cat, you'll see him cunningly withdraw.

Othello is a family bird; he's widely known as such
And, though of regal origin, he has the common touch.
In springtime, like his subjects, he engages in the strife
(But he with such an appetite) to woo and win a wife.
With kingly condescension he allows his chosen bride
To build the nest herself and hatch the eggs she lays inside.
He much prefers to feed his brood on worms his vassals slay
Which he accepts as tribute (when their heads are turned away.)
His offspring, once matured, arrives the time for them to go
And, if it breaks the royal heart, he doesn't let it show; Indeed,
he takes it on himself to help them on their way. Their
pleadings notwithstanding that they'd really rather stay.

*

Othello is a memory now; I'll never see him more.
For all that marked his passing was a patch of royal gore.
His palace stands unoccupied and few will venture near.
And those who in bravado dare, soon hurry off in fear.
The birds who land to search for food are always ill at ease,
Perhaps they sense a Presence there, where I but feel the breeze.
Today I watched them forage where Othello used to tread
And, apprehensive though they were, they bathed and preened and fed
Then, suddenly, they all uprose, as with a common will
And, shrieking, hurtled from my sight, then everything was still.
I scanned the garden, mystified, and in the hawthorn tree
I saw a small albino bird – or so it seemed to me.

THE MAKING OF MAN

Almighty God,
When asked by an inquisitive bod
Just why he made man from the slime
Replied, "'It seemed a good idea at the time."

ACTION REPLAY

One night behind the ruined shed
I met my lover, Penny Head;
I'd longed to touch those comely hips
And taste those pretty pouting lips,
Yet we just smiled and never spoke,
But I was blushing when I woke.

The second night we met again
But then I played the ardent swain;
I boldly kissed those luscious lips
And held unchecked those witching hips
Then – oh! – too soon the morning broke,
But I was panting when I woke.

The third night by the ruined shed
I found her parents there instead.
They called me libertine and cur
And asked what my intentions were
Then both of them began to cry;
I woke before discov'ring why.

1 dreamed no more of Penny Head
And trysts behind the ruined shed.
We both were then of tender years
Though more developed than our peers;
But still my glass I fondly raise
To Kindergarten!
Happy days!

MY FACE

I'm weary and worn with it
And wish I could change it
Alas I was born with it
And can't unarrange it.

I bear not the brunt of it
So I shouldn't mind it;
It's you who're in front of it -
I'm here safe behind it!

IT'S ALL RIGHT FOR YOU, COCK.

I watch a cocky blue tit ply
His acrobatics;
And think he wouldn't be so spry
With my rheumatics.

AT THE THEATRE

(Don't mind me - I'm only here for the play.)

The chap who comes in late
Is always garrulous and inebriate;
And though he can only stagger to his seat
He's an expert at making stepping-stones of everybody's feet
.

He sits in the middle of a row as a matter of course
And tends to breathe like an asthmatic horse.

He is leery and ill-mannered
And his breath is beery and well-Havana-ed.

He waits until he is seated before he laments
That he has neglected to go beforehand to the gents.
So, using the stepping-stones once more,
He performs an unrequested encore.

When he returns, he talks like a Stentor to a neighbour
About the virtues of voting Conservative or Labour;
And insists that she accepts a cigar and a swig of rum
As a sign of friendship until Kingdom come.

He asks her a series of questions
Which might be construed as improper suggestions;
But when she tries to quieten him in a friendly fashion
It is she who is made the object of everyone else's passion.

He always brings boiled sweets in a bag that rustles,
Reminiscently of a roomful of ladies wearing heavily starched
        bustle
And he sucks them in a manner unbecoming
So that the manager is seen looking for faulty plumbing.
He is skilled in the art of spilling his sweets onto the floor
And in exhorting his neighbours not to rest until they are in his
        bag once more.

He assists them with his cigarette-lighter which hisses and flashes
And threatens to reduce the theatre to a heap of rubble and ashes.

However, this disturbance does not continue until the end of
        the play
This is not because the sober patrons complain
And the manager sends him home again
But because he usually falls asleep in Act One and slides
        beneath the stalls
And stays that way until Act Two when the curtain falls.

What I can't understand is this: Is it accident or design
That the fellow always contrives to book the seat next to mine?

LIGHTS OUT

I'll have to switch it off
Mum's already called out
And she's bound to check
Trouble is
Coming back from the switch
It'll be pitch black
And that's when he'll strike
If he's here tonight
And I'll bet my bike he is.

O'course
If Mum has to switch it off
It's problem solved
 But I'll get bawled out.

He's not behind the door
Nor under the bed
I've looked
But best be sure

Right then
Ready to run for it
One - two
(It was ten last night)
Three – four – GO
O.K.
Can't stop for the chest
Nor the chair
Take a chance

Switch off
No-one there
Off – on – off – on –
Blind him. with science
Off – on – off – on – GO

One – two – three
Jump for it
Under the sheet
Down in the bed
Feet – feet – keep 'em in
If he has 'em.
You're dead

Thumpetty heart tonight
But it's quiet out there
Too quick for him all right
And it's safe down here
Any way – I don't scare
No bloody fear

NEIGHBOUR HOODS

When my neighbours have their grandchildren to stay
I invariably shout hip-hip-hooray.
Not because they're nice kids and impeccably behaved;
They're not. They're irreversibly depraved.
I speak the truth and nothing but the truth
When I say they're uncouth and nothing but uncouth,
Except when they are being noisy as well, and aggressive and
        fractious,
For which their grandparents ought to be more repressive and
        whacktious.
If they were in the world as a result of *my* son plighting his troth
I wouldn't admit it – even on oath.

Their favourite game is attempting to murder each other
While the victim screams for father or mother;
The idea is, firstly, to see who can get nearest to committing
        slaughter
Without actually completing it; in fact, stopping just shaughter;
And, second, to see who can scream loud enough for the
        parents to hear
Even though they are in Outer Mongolia or Tanzania.
But the parents will only be driven back by famine or drought.
Hoping, in the meantime, their kids will have cancelled each
        other out.

Another game for which they have a considerable bent
Is demolishing their grandparents' hereditament.
This is usually played while I am taking my nap post-prandial,
And they do it by blasting the walls with transistorised music
        sforzandial,
And attacking the structure by slamming doors con fuoco
Then waiting for the place to fall apart poco a puoco.
Complete collapse they would regard as an achievement
Particularly if it were accompanied by a bereavement.

But why, you may ask, do I, a lover of solitude and quiet,
Always cheer when the kids arrive for this festival of mayhem
        and riot?
Because the waiting for them to come is at an end
And in a week silence will again descend.
You see, my friends, I love beyond all else the serenity
I know I'll have when they return their progeny.
It is like the peace of God in the Bible –
It passeth understanding and is indescribible.

(The scriptural allusion comes from Philippians.)
Farewell, kids, and hip-hip-hippians!

TEMPTATION

To happiness I've found the key;
No longer doth it lie concealed.
Whenever Satan tempteth me –
I yield.

PSYCHOLOGY

"The noise from your neighbour's has stopped then," I said.
And old Sammy replied with a nod of his head.
"But what happened?" I asked (I was anxious to know); "You
were almost demented a fortnight ago."

"And that wasn't without a good reason," said he.
"There's not much that depresses or irritates me.
But that wireless of his with its boom and its blare
In the end even I didn't know how to bear.

My wife went to speak to him but, at the time,
So intense was the volume she had to use mime –
But he couldn't make out what she'd tried to convey
So he tapped on his temple and waved her away.

Well the noise didn't stop so I called the Police
And a constable warned him of breaching the peace,
And he spoke about covenants, customs and law.
Then he left – but I'm sure it was worse than before.

But it seems that he asked for the vicar to call
And with him it was Moses, commandments and Paul,
And Adam and Eve and original sin.
(He was shouting throughout to compete with the din.)

Then I had an Inspector of Health on the case
Who delivered a lecture on volume and space.
And decibels, logs and their bases of ten
And how x over five was a factor of n.

Then *he* sent a neighbourhood worker around
Who wasn't upset in the least by the sound;
In fact she went in and decided to stay
And she sang to his wireless the rest of the day!

But as soon as she left him I barged through the door
And I struck his machine from its stand to the floor;
And I said it had driven me all but insane.
And I didn't intend it would do so again,

So if ever things came to a similar pass
He'd be feeling my boot from his teeth to his ass;
And since then it's been still as the grave, as you've heard.
"That's psychology," Sammy explained "In a word!"

GREENBOTTLES

They buzz and sound so discontented
And on occasions quite demented.
But would you laugh if your cognomen
Disclosed the shade of your abdomen?

DON'T BLAME ME – DARWIN STARTED IT

Her course above the field a cuckoo plied,
Until she found a nest but lately made
With pipit's eggs reposing deep inside.
She added one to those already laid,
Then from her eye as she prepared to go
A watcher may have seen a tear ooze out
And heard her say, "I hate behaving so
But that's what evolution's all about!"

Before that bird departed, from the nest
The pipit's eggs she studied thoughtfully
Then gathered up the brightest and the best
And took the booty to a nearby tree.
She then devoured it avidly, although
A watcher might have seen a tear ooze out
And heard her say, "I hate behaving so
But that's what evolution's all about!"

When soon the cuckoo nestling burst its shell
 It turned its sightless eyes towards the brood;
Its fearful gaze betokened twice a knell
And, while parents foraged round for food,
It heaved the nestlings to the ground below.
A watcher may have seen a tear ooze out
And heard it say, "I hate behaving so
But that's what evolution's all about!"

A magpie later chanced to pass that way
And saw the cuckoo nestling waxing fat.
And, while the pipits sought their prandial prey,
He thought he'd make a mid-day meal of that;
The which he did with minimum of fuss.
Although one may have seen a tear ooze out
And heard him say, "I hate behaving thus
But that's what evolution's all about!"

The nestling cuckoo's mother, by the way.
Had found a reed-bed and a warbler's nest.
And there a second egg proposed to lay;
But neighbours mobbed the uninvited guest
And forced her to a watery tomb below.
Awash, she may have seen their tears ooze out
And heard them say, "We hate behaving so
But that's what evolution's all about!"

FAIR PLAY

Consider Pearl and Ernie Blake;
Her theme for concord – give and take,
And all the while their marriage lives
So Pearl will take while Ernie gives.

SONNET

(Abbreviated version of Keats' Ode To a Grecian Urn)

Thou still unravished bride of quietness,
Thou foster-child of silence and slow time.
Sylvan historian, who canst thus express
A flowery tale more sweetly than our rhyme:

Fair Youth, beneath the trees, thou canst not leave
Thy song, nor ever can those trees be bare;
Bold lover, never, never canst thou kiss
Though nigh those witching lips, – yet do not grieve;
She cannot fade, though thou hast not thy bliss;
Forever wilt thou love and she be fair.

Ah, happy, happy boughs that cannot shed
Thy leaves, nor ever bid adieu the spring;
And happy melodist unwearied
For aye –

   Oh, damn!

     I've dropped the bloody thing!

OGDEN NASH, THE WOMBAT AND ME

Although I'd love to write some lines about the wombat
I feel I must forsake it;
To rhyme my Muse can only offer combat
And Ogden Nash bespake it.

Of course I could employ marsupial.
And then, like Ogden, play with it,
E.G. say it's antipodupial
But *I'd* not get away with it.

Nor telling how this beast nocturnal
In Britain felt a failure
So tunnelled through the lands infurnal
To pop up in Austrailure.

I'll never write about the wombat
Nor paint his portrait in gouache;
And I'll not join in mortal combat
With anyone called Ogden Nache.

PROMISES, PROMISES

The bakery promised to cater for rakes;
On the door it said NAUGHTY BUT NICE.
But I found it referred to the cream-covered cakes
And not to Miss Grimm and Miss Grice.

THE TALE OF PASSER DOMESTICUS

I see two sparrows on my lawn;
The one, a cock-bird in his prime,
Towards the other helpless drawn
By instincts primitive as time;

But she, a hen, seems unaware
A passioned suitor circles round
And downward looks with studious air
Inspecting morsels on the ground.

But, resolute, the lusty male
Still nearer hops to gain the prize
With drooping wings, an upturned tail
And noisy, shrill, insistent cries.

The hen looks up and catches sight
Of that cavorting cock at last;
She pecks his head then takes to flight –
But not too far and not too fast.

She lights by my savoys in fact
To where her suitor whisks his way;
And, plainly well-rehearsed, they act
The scene that ends their little play.

I stand a while and contemplate
How sparrows human beings match;
Though I don't think I'd consummate
My marriage in a cabbage patch.

TRAGEDY AT CHRISTMAS

My Aunt Jemima died on Christmas Eve
From drinking too much whisky, I believe.
Her husband, Horace, hung his hoary head
And weeping uncontrollably he said,
"It's – oh – so sad – I don't know what I'll do –
I bought a chicken big enough for two!"

TRIPLE BUFFET

Two members of my family,
My Uncle Bob and cousin Bea
Both died within a week or so
And scarcely were they laid below
Before a third was stricken down –
This time my aunt, Eliza Brown.

I took this triple buffet hard –
I'd bought each one a Christmas card
Which meant (at thirty pence times three)
I'd wasted all of ninety p.

My brother urged me to be brave
And think of all the stamps I'd save,
But this a certain logic lacked
For he, of course, ignored the fact
That savings though there'd plainly be
They'd still be less than ninety p.

But when the problem I'd explained
He said (if just a little pained)
"Well, send the cards that they'll have missed
To others on your Christmas list!"
"I can't," I cried "I need no more
As everyone is catered for!"

"So then," said he, "your course is clear;
You use the cards another year!"
"Oh, that," I told him, "would be bliss
Except I've dated them for this!"

No ready answer could he find
And turned the matter in his mind.
Then said at length, "I've found the key;
Next Christmas, you send one to me
And why not use the other two
For my twin daughters, Di and Sue?
You'd only have to change the date
Or write instead 'Regret I'm late.'"
And though this remedy implied
My ninety pence remaining tied
For twelve months longer (and a bit)
I didn't care to mention it;
Nor ask what next year I should do
If they were dead and buried too.

EPITAPH ON A LOUD-MOUTH

Marcus Barker's
Carcase.
Starkers.

THE BELOVED

He took the mirror
Without demur
And clearly accustomed to the task
Held it level with her face
Full and softly freckled
Inching backwards towards the kerb
Until checked by a curt nod

He ignored the nudges and taunts
Of passers-by
As she combed her copper hair
Unhurriedly
Stepping forward from time to time
Tongue clicking
To readjust the mirror
In his drooping hand
And rouse him from the reverie
Of one before a Rembrandt

Satisfied at last
She took back the mirror
And returned it with the comb
To her tan-coloured handbag

He picked up her violin case
Put a protective arm about her
And crossed the road
By the pelican lights

He removed it
Only as they passed beneath an arch
Bearing the legend
St. Paul's Primary School – Pupils.

THE CHOW-CHOW

A Mongolian dog is the chow-chow;
It was shipped to the West from Macao-cao,
Not using the junk.
Which might well have sunk
But the scow-scow, the dhow-dhow and how how!

LET'S GO ROUND AGAIN

A virgin first God made
Then following a whim
He fecundated her
And she gave birth to him.

THE SONNET BEAUTIFUL

Shakespearean sonnets from my pen have flowed
Adown the years, and yet it were pretence
To claim that e'en the best became the mode
Beloved of Avon's ageless eminence.

But one abided, so refined and rare,
Though pent, unwrit, within the depths of me
That men would long have knowledged me his heir
Had I but found the clew to set it free.

Then yesternight – unbid but welcome guest! –
It came complete before me as I slept;
My Sonnet Beautiful, my soul's bequest,
The passion so profound, I woke and wept.

But publication needs must be deferred –
I can't recall a single, bloody word.

IF...

If you've been in the lair
Of a sore-headed bear
And studied kung-fu and karate;
If you've struggled for life
With a cannibal's wife
And you've been to an Acid House party;

If you lived through the Blitz,
Clung on to your wits
And you've undergone S.A.S. training;
If you've been at Heathrow
In a strike or go-slow
And you've gone on your way uncomplaining;

If you fought in the war
Faced the Afriker Corps
And outwitted Sardinian banditti;
If you've scrummed it at rugger
And mastered a mugger –
Then you're fit for the sales in the City.

BRIEF ENCOUNTER

(Black widow spider)

He dates with her,
She meets him.
He mates with her,
She eats him.

BLOW-FLY

A blow-fly's buzz disturbs the calm;
I fling the frontal casements wide.
And though I wish the thing no harm,
I'd much prefer she rasp outside.

But hardly is the exit clear
Before the creature flies pell-mell
Towards the window at the rear;
I open that one wide as well.

A draught upsets the letter-rack;
My papers scatter everywhere.
I pick them up. I twist my back.
I strike my head against my chair.

The noise has stopped. She's gone I think.
I quickly pull the casements to.
A panel cracks. I pour a drink.
I sit. The whining starts anew;

She's flying round the bonsai tree,
The lampshade next and then the door.
I open it. She passes me.
I curse the fly. I'll take no more.

I feel aggressive now – and mean.
She's had her chance to fly away.
I seize a glossy magazine.
I fold it and I stalk my prey.

I strike and find she isn't there.
I try again and hit a plate,
A lamp, a vase. I thrash the air.
I give up – and deliberate.

She's probably a female fly
Who needs to lay her eggs in haste
And looked in here when passing by –
To find a piece of meaty waste.

I can afford, if that is so.
To slight this blue barbarian; –
And even laugh. She doesn't know
That I'm a vegetarian!

BLACKBERRYING

Though the thorns on the briars your task may bedevil,
The uppermost fruit should be docked.
Their flavour is sweeter than those on the level
Where the leg of a dog may be cocked.

THE REVOLVING YEAR

You mustn't miss our New Year Sale,
Of course it's on the grandest scale,
You might well find the Holy Grail –
There's everything inside;
And why not travel overseas?
Just send a large deposit please,
And fly by Jumbo to Belize
Or cross the Great Divide.

For votaries of Valentine –
A published, passioned PLEASE BE MINE!
It's only twenty quid a line
(With payment in advance);
You'll need a card for Mothers' Day
A bowl of fruit, a fine bouquet –
And why not see a West End play
Or take a trip to France?

Do have a juicy, turkey-steak,
An Easter- egg,
A simnel cake –
And try a Continental Break
With free-of-duty liquor;
A day with Debbie must be won –
You'll find your coupon in the Sun –
And don't forget a hot-cross bun
And offerings for the vicar.

A Whitsun wedding's sheer delight,
The groom in black, the bride in white,
And if you find that money's tight –
Just sign here, sir and ma'am;
Remember, too, while you're away
To buy a gift for Fathers' Day –
A snooker set, a new toupee
Or send a Kiss-O-Gram.

The August holidays are here
And posters BACK TO SCHOOL appear
And GIFTS AND GOODS REDUCED TO CLEAR
Are everywhere about.
The catalogues drip through your door
With glossy photographs galore
Of things you didn't know before
You couldn't live without.

It's time for fetes and bargain buys.
For Trick-Or-Treat and pumpkin pies
And twenty p. for tawdry guys
(Inflation, mister – sorry !)
Then bearded gentlemen arrive
To start the Christmas selling drive
And soon it's carols – taped, not live.
And broadcast from a lorry.

If English Christmases offend
Allow me, sir, to recommend
You book a break with us and spend
The week in New South Wales;
But do make sure you're back betimes
For Hogmanay and New Year chimes,
The circuses, the pantomimes –
And January Sales.

HEIR TO THE POETIC TRADITION – WELL NEARLY

I think with pride and yet humility,
Whilst sitting at my desk to write my lay.
The self-same sun that sheds its light on me
Illumined too the cot of Mr Gray.

My pen I take from its accustomed place,
I collocate a sheaf of virgin sheets.
The while acutely conscious I may trace,
In my procedures, those of Mr Keats.

And as upon the Muse I trembling wait
My soul receptive and suffused with hope,
It thrills me throughly as I contemplate
That likewise sat and waited Mr. Pope.

I meditate a while within my bower;
Alas, Euterpe will not come today.
I give up after doodling for an hour –
So unlike Messrs. Pope and Keats and Gray.

345, 346, 347...

To cure insomnia I've tried
By counting sheep as they bestride
A rustic gate that stands beside
A beck.

But even that keeps me awake
And causes head and heart to ache
For fear a sheep should slip and break
Its neck.

HELP!

Carrot-flies live on carrots.
Parrot-flies live on parrots.
Dragon-flies have a problem.

LIFE OF RILEY

I'm sorry for young Paul who lives across the road from me;
He's ill, although I've no idea what's wrong;
He's wan and wasted, bent and slow – it's pitiful to see, –
He used to be so upright, spry and strong.

His wife, Rebecca, left him for a barrister at Slough,
And that's to blame to some extent I'd say;
His job's demanding too, although he doesn't travel now –
He's worked at home since Becky went away.

I've never known quite what he does – it's all a mystery.
He's often working far into the night;
I sometimes go to bed as late as half past two or three
And his bedside lamp will still be burning bright.

It worried me at first when Becky left him on his own.
Him working six or seven days a week;
He lost a lot of weight – must have dropped to seven stone –
And now is so unkempt where once he was so sleek.

At least there's someone there should he collapse or even worse
A secretary's with him all the day;
Another comes most evenings, though she might well be a nurse,
She seems to work or watch the night away.

WHO'S BEEN A NAUGHTY GIRL, THEN?

"You ought to know," the airman read,
"While you're in Greenland based,
Your fiancée is being —well –
To say the least – unchaste."

The letter was anonymous.
He didn't know who'd shopped her;
But he flew home to check the tale
And – oh! – by helicopter.

LETTER FROM AMERICA

The advertisement called it THE LAND OF THE FREE
But I think it was some sort of joke
Or a piece of commercial extravagance
I've been *here* for a week and I'm broke!

TO BE OR NOT TO BE

I wish I were a snail
With countless kin my dowry –
The necklace-shell, the eolid.
The cuttlefish, the clam, the squid.
The oyster and the cowry.

Oh, a snail's life for me.
No fixed abode to bind me;
So if I felt by neighbours pent
I'd take up my hereditament
And leave them all behind me.

I wish I were a snail.
No need for cash or credit;
No charge for breakfast, dinner, tea,
Accommodation furnished free –
Just me to board and bed it.

Oh a snail's life for me
Where casual sex is normal;
And, as I'd be hermaphrodite,
Of anyone I'd take delight
With everything informal.

I wish I were a snail.
No more domestic friction;
No parent, daughter, son or spouse
To cause confusion in the house
And joy in contradiction.

But if I were a snail
My nerves might tear to tatters;
I'd live in dread of vulpine brutes.
Of hedgehogs, thrushes, gardeners' boots
And continental platters.

And if I were a snail
I'd have to change my diet
To mosses, fungi, rotten fruits.
Decaying earthworms, slugs and newts, –

I'm not inclined to triet!

ON THE VICAR'S WELL-BUILT SPOUSE

Mrs. Levy
Is top-heavy.

FROM PLAYFUL

TO

PENSIVE

HAPPY ARE THEY

Happy are they who first discover
A childhood friend is now their lover.
But happier they, when passions end,
Who in the lover find a friend.

OUTCAST

I heard the car door slam
The plaintive puzzled cry
The shriek of tyres
The car splashing through the night

And on my step at dawn
He sat soaked and shivering
His old and misty eyes
Searching mine

I'm not one for dogs I said
So you can't stay here
And you needn't stare like that
I'm immune.

I'll call the police
They'll dispose of you
Find a home or something
You can wait in the shed

But I didn't phone them straight away
And he spent the long months
Of a cruel winter
In front of my fire

Sprawled along the carpet
Chin on my slippers
Those old and misty eyes
Still searching mine

And lying there he closed them
In the last cold sleeping
Late home I found him
And guilty gently opened them

But in their soft sightless stare
I saw through my own
Old and misty eyes
No reproaches there.

LUCY

One loved you well when life was green
And still when it was grey;
Had he but spoken, you but seen,
You might have shared the years between
And known no bitter day.

But young, you left us – not for fame,
Though that before you lay,
But then you chose to yield your name
And trust that fledgling heart and frame
To one of worthless clay.

He said he loved you, but he lied;
You were but helpless prey.
His practised arts he smoothly plied
Until you walked with him a bride,
Unblemished as the may.

And on that earliest marriage-bed
When tense and torn you lay,
You weren't the first, he'd vaunting said,
Nor would be last though you were wed –
And yet you chose to stay.

You'd promised in that holy place
To keep to him, you'd say;
But was it for the taunting face
The faithless heart and brute embrace
You gave yourself that day?

We longed for him to loose your chain,
His former vows unsay;
And, rid of rancour, rue and pain.
You'd learn to live and laugh again
With none to give you nay.

But came that thief while lone you slept
Who bears the breath away;
And, saddened, we who loved you wept,
But he that night had elsewhere kept
Nor came to where you lay.

But one who loved when life was green
And still when it was grey,
A crimson rosebud left unseen
To tell of all that might have been
If you had looked his way.

BILLIE

(To the memory of William, Beagles M.M.)

A farmer's boy before the call
To fight the war to end them all,
He'd heard of glory, king and God
But never of the blood-stained sod,
The stench of death, despair and dread.
"They might have told me," Billie said.

The sergeant said, "If you believe
Those letters strapped around your sleeve
Mean Stretcher-Bearer – you've been 'ad.
They stand for Silly Bugger, lad.
You're down to work in muck and mire.
Untangle corpses on the wire
And 'ump 'em back be'ind the line
And just as likely crack your 'ead."
"They might have told me," Billie said.

"You see that mound up on the right?"
They asked him in the fading light.
A man lies hurt below the brow;
You fetch 'im in – it's quiet now –."
Above the trench he looked around
Then crawled across the cratered ground
To see, through grimed and smarting eyes,

Beneath a sudden, hostile flare,
Not one, but two men lying there.
The nearer spoke, "Are you alone?
I'm lame, boy, and I'm fourteen stone.
This poor sod's stopped a load of lead."
"They might have told me, "Billie said.

But straightway bent his sturdy back
And on his shoulder, like a sack,
He lodged the lame man and, as calm,
He locked the other in his arm;
Then through the murk and sucking mire,
The flickering flares and sniper-fire,
With not a thought to bow or blench
He trudged tenacious toward the trench.

They said the lame man soon would mend;
The other's war was at an end –
An hour they reckoned he'd been dead.

"He might have told me,'' Billie said.

ACROSS THE HEARTH

Though bewildered by years
He knew love yet
And spoke its precious idioms
Across the hearth
Whose fire first blushed
When love was fresh
And glowed warm still
Constant as he

But no response came
No murmured communion

His eyes moist
Sought the faded photograph
Solitary over the fireplace
Where a bride looked out timid
On her later unremembering self.

But he who stood beside her proud
Remembered

He turned back
To two uninhabited eyes
Drifting in a void
Inaccessible

And there was silence still
Save that the fire sighed

TO THOSE WHO LIE WHERE FRUIT TREES GROW

(Gressenhall Rural Life Museum was once a workhouse. There is a burial-plot within the grounds where many of the inmates were interred from a re-usable coffin. There are no headstones above the graves nor, when I enquired, are there records within the museum of those lying there. The burial-ground was closed in 1900 and an orchard now covers the site.)

In bleak November there's a solemn hour
When but a bugle-call, a doleful bell
And stifled sobs disturb the hush that shrouds
The village churchyard and the city square
As those who stand remember those who fell.

Unknowing that the rage of war is done,
The slain from ancient battlefields sleep on
Where simple headstones mark each alien bed,
While monuments on distant, dearer soil
Tell where they walked once, toiled and wed.

But you, cast crudely in this lowly place
Into the naked embrace of cold clay,
Have no memorial here or otherwhere,
And only bones, betrayed where badgers delve,
Bear witness that you passed this way.

Yet you fought too, though not with human foe;
Your brutal battleground was life itself
Where, thrust, you strove for year on weary year
Fiercely as any soldier in the field
Until, strength spent, you yielded here.

But on your beds, unmarked when first you slept.
Now rooted well within them, fruit trees grow;
And when among those living monuments,
I saw a figure standing, still, head bared
As others stand on bleak November days
I wished that you could know.

BESIDE THE YEW

(To the memory of Lister Leville)

I couldn't have known
Little brother
When our mother said
You'd gone for a ride
It would end here
Beside the yew

I was only three then
And you not two
Though you've not aged
As I and this old tree

And down the years
The sun has never set
But I think on that day

Uncle Bill and Aunt Jane were there
So it could have been Christmas again
Except that the curtains were not drawn back
And nobody laughed anymore
And I was taken next door to play.

They said you'd been ill
But I knew that
The night you went so chill
After you'd coughed and cried
In such a curious way

And when I woke
You weren't there
And mother said
The doctor had taken you away
To sleep in another bed
I cried as well

In the morning when you went for that ride
Aunt Jane said
I would see you again
One day.

It was kindly meant
Though I knew she lied
Yet here I am.
A foolish old fellow
But hoping like that boy
Of sixty years ago
That it might be so.

ANNIVERSARY

My husband said this morning as he woke,
"I love you, Jo."
And that meant more than when at first he spoke
Fifty years ago.

THE OLD SOLDIER

The freckled face
Not unlike his own
Was staring up at the solitary silver medal
Gleaming in the glass case
Beside a framed photograph
Faded, pierced and stained

It was my reward
For killing a man I didn't know
The old soldier said

Two years before
We'd have passed each other in the street
With a nod of the head
And p'r'aps a good morning
But we were on the Somme
And it was war

He was in a machine-gun nest
Last man left alive
But my bullets had gone when we met

They pinned that medal on me
Because I got in first with my bayonet

No
I never wear it
It belongs there
With that old photograph
It's what the medal cost…

No
It's just that my eyes are sore today
Old soldiers don't cry boy…

You can hardly make it out now
But it shows a boy a bit like you
Except that he was on the enemy's side
And he lost his dad in the war

It was in his breast pocket

OLD TOM

At first we passed each other by
With just a nod, Old Tom and I,
But then he called – a curious cry –
"Well met!" he said, "Well met!"
And after that he'd often stay
To talk a while, but soon he'd say,
"It's late, my friend, I must away –
I fear my wife will fret."

His boots had long since lost their sheen,
His overcoat was old and mean,
His hat a faded, pitted green,
His body bowed with years.
The stubble sprouted on his chin,
The blood lay hid beneath his skin,
The chestnut eyes were blurred within
And often touched with tears.

Yet though by time Old Tom was tried
By poverty he could not hide
And private sorrows but implied
He never owned regret;
But pensive he'd become each day
Before he raised his hat to say,
"It's late, my friend, I must away, –
I fear my wife will fret."

***

I see him in the lane no more.
Uneasy neighbours forced the door
And found him huddled on the floor.
They told me of his life.
The house was where he'd brought his bride
And where, too frail to bear, she'd died;
Alone since then he'd never tried
To win a second wife.

His course on earth had all but sped
And yet he knew me by the bed.
The mutely moving lips I read;
"Well met" they said. "Well met!"
He closed his eyes and smiling lay.
Then distantly I heard him say,
"It's late, my friend, I must away –
Tonight she shall not fret."

AT THE WAR MEMORIAL

"They gave their lives for country, King and God
In glorious sacrifice ..." the statesman said;
But from afar, beneath a foreign sod
There came a murmur from a host long dead.

And one there cried, "I did not <u>give</u> my life.
Too dear it was that I should freely yield.
A stranger stole it with his thrusting knife
And left me stark and still on Flanders Field."

"In peace a pauper – country, King and God
Cared naught for me and mine," another said.
"Came war and I was courted, clothed and shod
And put to work at slaughter for my bread."

A third voice cried, "The shell that took my life
And widowed one I'd lately left a bride
Was made by men whose profit lay in strife
And in that selfsame land for which I died."

Then spoke a fourth, "Not glorious sacrifice.
I foully slew and foully I was slain;
And loth was I to pay that cruel price
And quit the world – though it no longer sane."

A fifth, crushed by slaughter, slime and stench,
Told of a churchyard, rope and kindly yew;
A sixth of standing clear above his trench
And, dying, blessing one he never knew.
The last said, "Never met those in the fight
Whose greed and folly set the world aflame
But humbler men, who knew not hate or spite,
Yet, would they live themselves, must kill and maim."

But deaf the statesman stood beside the stone
To those who long in alien soil had slept;
But some there heard – gaunt women, grey and lone.
And men, bemedalled, bent – who, silent, wept.

LORRAINE

My heart was discovered, its secret confessed,
But the love it had told she dismissed as a jest;
She brushed me aside and disdainfully smiled –
For she was a woman and I but a child.

I struggled, but vainly, to hold back my tears
And I fled with her ridicule racking my ears;
Oh! The void when a love is rebuffed and reviled
By a woman who captures the heart of a child!

The distance between us I swore I would span
Though it took till I spoke with the voice of a man;
But too soon had my goddess another beguiled –
And he was her groom and I still a child.

But he looked not a year on Lorraine as a wife
For the breath of their baby was bought with her life;
And all wondered that weeping was never so wild, –
How little they knew of the heart of a child!

I lavished my love on her daughter instead
And many a time as an infant she said,
"Will you marry me soon?" Oh, so artlessly styled!
And I wept when alone for that motherless child.

As a woman her question continues the same.
But I know that I never can give her my name;
For what if her body by mine were defiled
If I thought it another's I'd loved as a child?

CARA

She steals into my solitude
Silent as drifting thistledown
And in the intimacy of night
Seals me in sleep with a whisper;

And though gone with the waking
The brush of her breath on my cheek
The face pale and chill as the pillow
No void I feel, no aching –

For, constant, she will come again
When slow day yields to kindly night.
Love such as early fused our flesh
Survives its passions – and its passing.

THE BATTLEFIELD

Time will renew this bleak landscape where men,
Strangers, who had no quarrel, fought and fell;
The shell-gashed field will heal, new trees flourish
And birds build in the branches.

But those who ceased here to be.
Lying broken now, scattered in cold clay.
Men who laughed and loved once and strode the earth strong –
They will never be renewed;

And the pale, black-clad pilgrims gathered close,
Alien in culture but kindred in grief,
Who bore them whole or who waited to bear,
Weep, bowed, knowing it is so.

OVER YONDER

(In a Lincolnshire churchyard)

Beside the gate my father spoke,
"They're over yonder by the oak."

Alone it stood, its boughs outspread
As if to bless the unnamed dead
At rest beneath its ivied shroud;
And though but strangers in that mould
I knew their blood had been endowed
To him and me through years untold.

His mother once had lived nearby
But, widowed young, went far away,
And I beneath a Fenland sky
Had never stood until that day;
Yet with that canopy of space
The stillness of that ancient place
And those who slept beneath the tree
I felt a strange affinity.

But how capricious then was I –
For when my father said that he
Must also over yonder lie
When soon or late he ceased to be,
I chided him for what I said
Was but a sentimental whim;
He had not known in life the dead
And nor had they, save one, known him.

Yet when I next stood by that gate
And turned my eyes from where but late
Another mound had been upthrown
Towards the boy whose tear-stained face
Bore, well-defined, the eye and bone
Of him new-resting in that place,
I said when he for me should weep
I too must over yonder sleep.

KISSES

I remember the kiss of a mother;
A stay for a timorous child;
A balm for the hurt of another
And a peace in a world that was wild.

And I think of the kiss of a father
And our solemn accord on the day
When, at seven, I said I would rather
Shake hands – in a dignified way.

In the deepest of memory's places
There's an old, unforgettable bliss
Of a sinewy arm that embraces
And a coveted, whiskery kiss.

I remember a sister who ended
The day with a kiss' and a yawn –
The tokens of battle suspended
Till the first of us woke with the dawn.

I think of a cousin who, dying,
Confessed with a kiss to a truth
Which her lips had till then been denying
That she'd loved from our earliest youth.

But the kiss of them all, the most tender,
Was the one in the eyes of Louise
That her lips were too proud to surrender –
And mine were too timid to seize.

TRANSFIGURATION

An old man is seated by the west door –
Of those stood altar-faced before him he knows best
The boy by the rood-screen
But the boy does not know him

Early sunbeams pour purple and gold and green
From the stained-glass Transfiguration scene
Over the boy
And beside him
His ample aunt romping through the processional hymn
Defying the dawdling organ

The old man sees
The boy's uncle nudge him in passing
A cousin wink from the choir-stalls
And Lame Joe the organ-blower
Child's mind confined in a full-grown frame
Play peekabo from behind his curtain

And he sees little Grace Hayward
Newly a bride
Who broke every lad's heart but one
And he beside her proud
Miss Brace the school-mistress
Prim with pince-nez and tightly packed bun
And Jim Joyce from the Jolly Farmers
Florid of face and wayward of voice

He knows the boy is with his own people again
And belongs here
Not in that drear smoke-steeped city
To others not his kin

An animated Amen and the old man sighs
Amen indeed
So let it be

*

Early women worshippers
See only an old man seated by the west door
Withdrawn and worn with days
They watch him dab distant eyes
Rise stiffly from his pew
And pass into the spring sunshine
A stranger

Lone he lingers in the stone-strewn churchyard
Still beneath a steepled poplar
And the women do not know
He is with his people again
Silent now
Sleeping in the kindly Fenland earth

SEASONS

In spring, as proud
Our love we told;
To cleave we vowed
Till hearts were mould.

And as we swore
So did we bide.
And loved the more
At summer-tide.

As autumn passed
So passion too;
But love held fast
Unaltered, true.

In winter, old
And lone I lie;
Does she sleep cold –
Or is it I?

IN THE FACE OF THE ENEMY

(In memorium O.W.T.)

"Some men who suffered the ultimate penalty for cowardice in the face of the enemy, would have made no claim they were heroes in the first place; others were heroes who turned away from, carnage they could no longer bear." (Royan Judge)

You did not flinch from brutal strife
Of other's ancient hatreds born;
Though choked by gas and gored by knife
You did not flinch.

You did not flinch when others fled
From taking up one close to death;
Through snipers' bullets spitting sped
You did not flinch.

You did not flinch, the battle gaine,
From turning slaughter-sate away;
Though life the forfeit fell ordained
You did not flinch.

You did not flinch the foe before
Nor, fettered, facing silent friends;
Though on your breast their barrels bore
You did not flinch.